Creation
versus
Evolution

New Scientific Discoveries

Investigation of the Evidence

Ralph O. Muncaster

Published by:

Strong Basis To Believe

Mission Viejo, California 92691

Creation
versus
Evolution

New Scientific Discoveries

Investigation of the Evidence

By Ralph O. Muncaster

A Special Thanks...

...To Mark Ritter for his technical editing assistance. Mark holds B.S. and M.S. degrees from Cal Poly Pomona with emphasis in chemistry. He has taught various courses in science including chemistry and astronomy. Mark is an apologetics correspondent for *Reasons To Believe*, an organization devoted to examining the scientific accuracy of the *Bible (see references)*. He is also president and editor of *Sword and Spirit* ministry.

Published by:

Strong Basis To Believe

Mission Viejo, CA 92691 U.S.A.

Copyright © 1997 by Ralph O. Muncaster
First Printing 1997
Printed in the United States of America

ISBN 1-888904-20-8

Creation
versus
Evolution

New Scientific Discoveries
Investigation of the Evidence

Scientists Speak Out [16]

" With regard to the origin of life, science... positively affirms creative power."
Lord Kelvin - Established Thermodynamics as a science

" I find more sure marks of authenticity in the Bible than in any profane history whatsoever."
Sir Isaac Newton - Developed Laws of Motion, Calculus

" (It is) as difficult to understand a scientist who does not acknowledge the presence (of God)...
...as it is to comprehend a theologian who would deny the advances of science."
Wernher von Braun - Space Scientist, Past Director of NASA

Creation or Evolution?
Why is it Important?

Great intellects quarrel over it... Educators fight over it... Even car symbols vie for attention over it. Origin of life is an emotional topic.

Why?

In its simplest form we are comparing alternative *mechanisms* of the beginning of life. One is chance. The other is design. *Both* require faith. *Both* define a religious viewpoint. Yet, creation is sometimes rejected as "religion". *Random* life development (i.e. "Evolution") is not. Why... if *both* are really only "mechanism alternatives"? Emotion must stem from implications *beyond the mechanism alone* (perhaps the implications of "God"). Such emotional fear is a roadblock to discovering the real facts. It limits education and new knowledge.

Random chance implies NO ultimate purpose, NO divine authority and NO absolute morality. Yet, a purposeful designer might have a plan for his creation. For some, the perceived freedom that comes from random evolution may seem attractive (i.e. no accountability to "God," or no absolute moral standards). Yet, the implications beyond the "truth" of creation are enormous. And everyone may not be affected equally... making it more important than ever to know the facts.

Does evidence support evolution or creation?
Today, many of the world's most brilliant scientists
say NO to evolution, YES to creation.

Discoveries in the last few years add immense evidence for creation. Now, the elite of the scientific field - in microbiology, biochemistry, physics and applied mathematics - often favor creation as the probable alternative. Top scientists are reconsidering Creation & God.[1, 4, 20]

Today, we can evaluate the beginning of life with rapidly accumulating scientific knowledge. Unfortunately, the world is slow to respond. It may be years before it is finally taught in schools. Yet the facts are accurately summarized, without error, in the *Bible*. More importantly, the *Bible* contains answers to other *implications beyond creation alone*. It would be tragic to allow such "other implications" to stop us from learning the truth... a truth that could mean life or death... eternally.

The Key Issues

Was Creation a <u>chance</u> event, or by <u>design</u>?

How are we here? Why? Is there a God? Does he interact with the world or human beings? Does he communicate with us? If so, how?

Chance	Design	Issue
Earth Amazing coincidence randomly provides a precise environment statistically inconceivable (p. 22-23)	**Earth** A Creator directs events to provide a perfectly fine-tuned planet for life (p. 22-23)	Is There a God?
 First Living Cell In a period billions of times older than the universe is thought to be... random events miraculously piece together the first living cell. (p. 16-21)	 **First Living Cell** A Creator hand-crafts the building blocks for life and introduces the first life forms to planet Earth. (p. 16-21)	Did God Create Life?
 Cell to Man Needing an infinately long period... random mutations lead to vastly superior, more complex organisms until Man appears. (pp. 6-7, 12-13)	 **Cell to Man** Basic design is applied to unique living organisms - each capable of variations within its special reproducing "kind". (pp. 8-9, 12-13)	Did God Create Man?
 Man's Purpose None.	 **Man's Purpose** Man was created for a divine purpose. (p. 26)	Is God Involved with Man?
 Implication Life is meaningless. No hope for eternity. Live for today.	 **Implication** Life has meaning. Prepare for eternity. Seek God's communication. (p. 26)	What Is God's Message?

Evolution Definition

Evolution simply means *change*. But now in the broadest sense, it defines the change of life from early single celled life-forms to man. Key sub-definitions are: *Micro*evolution - change *within* a species; *Macro*evolution - change *between* species

Microevolution

Preprogrammed into the DNA of every living thing is a genetic code that defines it characteristics. The genetic code often contains both dominant and recessive traits. A person born with brown eyes might also have the (hidden) genetic code for blue eyes. Hence, brown eyed parents could produce a blue eyed child. And the recessive trait could be hidden for generations then suddenly appear.

Sometimes a favorable trait is so advantageous that it helps animals survive while those without it die. Darwin called that tendency "Survival of the Fittest" or natural selection. The famous "Peppered Moth" example is in many biology textbooks (see insert). Moths with the favorable characteristics survived while the others didn't. Hence the favorable genes were usually passed on. Less favorable "hidden" genes became rare with fewer surviving moths to pass them on.

Virtually all informed people who believe creation accept the concept of *Micro*evolution. It's part of God's amazing programing that allows species to adapt to changing circumstances (as in the Peppered Moth example).

Macroevolution*

The theory of *Macro*evolution misapplies some of the basic principles of *Micro*evolution. It assumes that favorable characteristics somehow develop to allow one species to turn into another (e.g. a fish to a bird).

Since scientists know that no existing DNA programming for a species change exists (e.g. bacteria doesn't contain DNA to be anything but bacteria), the idea of mutation was developed to explain how DNA might be altered. Supposedly, some input of energy (such

The Peppered Moth Example

In the 1850's, a village had many white peppered moths (98%) along with a few black ones. Birds could easily see and prey on the black moths which were visible against the "white" lichen-covered bark. Camouflaged white moths survived and passed on genetic traits.

Later, pollution killed the lichen exposing the dark bark. Within years, the population shifted to 98% dark moths. Natural selection allowed the "fittest" genetic trait to survive. But genetic options *within* the species never changed. No new species evolved. It just adapted.

as radiation) caused a series of favorable mutations that allowed simpler life forms to become much more complex. Supposedly, the "favorable mutation" was passed on to offspring. Problems with this theory have been clearly exposed with research using modern technology (summarized throughout this book). As a result, informed microbiologists now almost unanimously reject *Macro*evolution.

6   * Note: Throughout this text, the word "Evolution" will refer to *Macro*evolution unless otherwise specified.

The Evolutionary Model

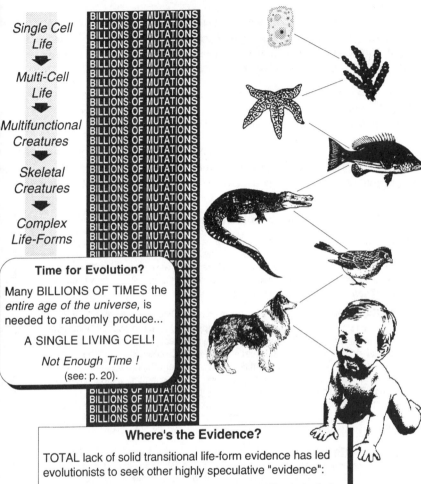

Single Cell Life
↓
Multi-Cell Life
↓
Multifunctional Creatures
↓
Skeletal Creatures
↓
Complex Life-Forms

BILLIONS OF MUTATIONS *(repeated)*

Time for Evolution?

Many BILLIONS OF TIMES the *entire age of the universe,* is needed to randomly produce...

A SINGLE LIVING CELL!

Not Enough Time !
(see: p. 20).

Where's the Evidence?

TOTAL lack of solid transitional life-form evidence has led evolutionists to seek other highly speculative "evidence":

1. Common Design? - This argument claims that "like design" of systems found in different animals (e.g. similar skeleton leg joints in bats, dogs and man) "prove" they evolved from a common ancestor. With such an argument, we might also conclude cars evolved from roller skates. Intelligent design applies good systems (e.g. a wheel) to various products.

2. Body-Part Remnants? - Many species have been examined for "useless" body parts that might imply some evolutionary heritage. The resulting "evidence" has led to findings later proving to be embarrassing. For example, evolutionists claimed the human fetus had vestiges of gills, a tail and a "yolk" sac. The "gill slits" are actually the canals that become the inner ear. The "tail" is the tailbone attachment point of muscles. The "yolk" sac is a vital source of the embryo's first blood cells.

Creation Definition

Creation is the belief that someone (or something?) created the universe and life as we know it. In essence, through a process unknown to us, God "spoke" (made to occur) all uniquely created objects into existence. Pre-programming by God (within DNA) allowed for reproduction of variations within "like kinds".

There is no evidence of <u>life</u> beyond what we know (p. 23). (There is, however, evidence of existence of spiritual beings in dimensions beyond space and time - as described in the *Bible* - beyond the scope of this book).

Creation, by definition, implies the existence of a "God" outside of our time-space dimension. Understanding dimensions beyond time and space also makes it easier to understand how God could create things in a seemingly miraculous way... and helps us recognize our child-like view of "God" and "miracles" (p 9).

Did God Create Everything in 6 Days?

An unfortunate disagreement among Biblical scholars is over the length of time it took God to complete creation (p. 10 - background history). One view is that God worked *within the known record of science* and that creation was in stages of billions of years (Old Earth). The other viewpoint is that creation took *6 literal days* (Young Earth). There are those who maintain both views.

<u>Old Earth View</u> (ref: 4, 19-25) - This view recognizes scientific evidence that the earth is billions of years old, and that man appeared on earth about 40,000 years ago. Recent scientific discoveries have so emphatically supported the *Bible* that it has caused many of the world's leading scientists to reconsider the God of the *Bible*. A perceived weakness of this view is in modern Biblical translations that use the words "day"... and "morning and evening " to describe the original creation timing. The original Hebrew words had multiple meanings ("yom" could have meant day or era. Similarly, words for morning and evening could have meant beginning and ending). The "Old Earth" creation view is 100% consistent with the *Bible*, when considering the original Hebrew writing.

<u>Young Earth View</u> (ref: 5, 6, 17, 26, 27) - This view argues that the *Bible* clearly indicates *6 literal 24-hour days*. Since the *Bible* itself is evidence of God's communication (ref: p. 28) it cannot be ignored. Some believe however, the view has inconsistencies with the scientific record (see "light" insert - p 19). Yet, obviously, a God of creation could have operated outside the laws of science or could have created things in an "aged" state. Jesus turned water into wine and multiplied bread and fish... both of which imply creation in an "aged" state.

All views: *Evolution, Old Earth* and *Young Earth* require a degree of faith. For *Evolution*, faith is in incredibly improbable chance. For *Old Earth Creation*, faith is in the *Bible* and its consistency with the scientific record. For *Young Earth Creation* faith is in the importance of semantic details within the *Bible*. Every person effectively makes a choice of where to place faith in the important creation question.

The *Bible* is <u>not</u> a book about <u>creation</u> nor about <u>science</u>. The important issue is not the *mechanism* nor *how long*... but *WHO*? The *Bible* refutes evolution since it clearly states that <u>GOD created</u> all species "out of nothing" (Hebrew - "*bara*"). *It does not deny, however, scientific mechanisms* (i.e. physics, chemistry or biology).

Understanding the Creation Miracle

A miracle is defined as something unexplainable by the laws of nature, thereby requiring a supernatural cause or God. Miracles generally fit into two categories:

1. **Miracles of Circumstance** - Something that works within the laws of nature that we know, yet is of miraculous timing or effect. Example: Hail decimates only the enemy during Joshua's battle of Gilgal [Josh 10:6-11].

2. **Miracles Beyond Known Physical Laws** - When something happens outside the known laws of physics. Example: Turning a staff into a snake [Ex 4:4] or water into wine [John 2:1-11].

The key to understanding miracles is recognizing that we are limited by the knowledge of dimensions of time and space that we live in. Except in mathematics, we can only speculate about dimensions outside the four in which we live. Obviously it's impossible to observe any scientific *laws* in dimensions beyond our own. Perhaps all miracles follow some "natural laws" in dimensions beyond time and space. Perhaps they don't. In either case, a God that could create the laws in the first place would certainly know how to work "outside of" or "around" them.

> **Quantum Physics Finds "Extra-Dimensions"**
>
> Latest breakthroughs in quantum physics indicate *at least 7 dimensions beyond time and space*. Scholars also calculate at least 7 extra dimensions in the *Bible*.[19]

Imagine a "3-D God"

One way to relate to the impact of extra dimensions is to imagine a world reduced to only two dimensions (like a tabletop). Imagine further, the existence of several tiny "flat" human beings. The "flatpeople" would view each other as only a line. They could get an idea of the total shape of each other only by moving around each other. They would NOT have the total view of a 3 dimensional observer.

Let's call such a 3 dimensional observer "3-D God". "3-D God" would be able to view an entire flatperson at once. Likewise, the "3-D God" could place a finger a fraction of an inch above a flatperson and the flatperson would never know he was there. "3-D God" would be totally invisible in the world of 2 dimensions, unless he chose to insert himself into it. By placing a finger on the 2 dimensional plane, "3-D God" would appear as one line to the flatpeople. Placing 3 fingers on the plane would appear as three lines. In either case, the flatpeople would have very little concept of the entire "3-D God". They might even be puzzled at how such a "3-D God" could exist as both one and three lines at the same time.

Likewise, the "3-D God" could know much more about a flat individual than the flatperson would know about himself. "3-D God" could also observe the totality of all flatpeople at once, even when the flatpeople were far apart. And "3-D God" could do things that would be considered miracles in the two dimensional space.

Such a simple illustration provides some insight of the impact of adding only one dimension. A real God existing in many dimensions outside of time and space could presumably produce incredible miracles beyond our understanding.

Historical Debate Over Creation

People are surprised when they learn that new technology provides *far more evidence of Creation* than ever before. Yet long before modern science, brilliant people including Newton, Galileo and Pasteur defended the *Genesis* account of creation. The *Bible* was the "most reliable authority" for centuries. In the United States, it became the first school textbook.

In the mid-1800's the advent of the theory of evolution and a coincident belief in "higher criticism" of the *Bible* initiated a century of doubt. Since then, modern archaeology and manuscript research have soundly refuted "higher criticism". Likewise, scientific breakthroughs have made a mockery of evolution. Unfortunately, misconceptions still abound in textbooks because evidence refuting errors is often "inadmissible" today - since it suggests "God". Hence it has become increasingly difficult to correct mistakes.

Darwin ignited the creation-evolution debate with his book *Origin of the Species* in 1859. The original publication openly acknowledged the necessity of God. The entire "molecules-to-man" idea occurred later. Creation or evolution events include:

Early Scholars - From Moses until the 1600's, the Biblical view of creation was considered fact. The *Genesis* account was taken very literally, and the *Genesis* "Creation-Day" was assumed to mean a period of time.

Geology - In the late 1700's to early 1900's recognition of fossils and study of rock layers led scholars to conclude that some chronology in creation was probable (we now know, it is exactly as described in *Genesis* p. 25). They further concluded it took place over a long period of time.

Wilberforce-Huxley Debate [1860] - An unprepared orator (Wilberforce - representing the *Bible*) was humiliated by a skilled scientist and orator (Huxley). This, combined with Darwin's book, shaped public opinion portraying Biblical scholars as prejudiced, uniformed and ignorant.

Scopes Monkey Trial [1925] - The conflict between the *Bible* and evolution peaked with a debate between William Jennings Bryan and defense attorney Clarence Darrow. Using information we now recognize as incorrect, Darrow forced Jennings to conclude the *Genesis* account could not have been literally accurate. The defeat had far reaching impact. It created a world perception that evolution was fact, forming a great barrier between the *Bible* and what was perceived as science. It also fueled a dispute between Young Earth/Old Earth scholars - which still needlessly hinders communication of the modern scientific support of the *Bible* today.

Einstein's General Relativity [1919+] - Einstein tried hard to exclude creation implications (God) from his own discoveries... Einstein eventually accepted that General Relativity implied a beginning (and even God).

1990's Breakthroughs - Recent discoveries supporting creation are rapidly expanding in all scientific fields including physics, microbiology, chemistry and anthropology.

Event	Date
Moses writes *Genesis*	1500
Septuagint, Dead Sea Scrolls Immortalize *Genesis*	250
Christ Confirms *Genesis*	0 / 30
Early Church	400
Advent of Geology	1700
Darwin	1859
Wilberforce Huxley Debate	1860
Einstein	1919
Scopes Trial	1925
Hubble	1929
Molecules to Man	19
COBE Sat.	
Hubble Tel.	
Quantum Physics	19

Intuition... Supports Creation

Recognizing that creation is more reasonable than evolution is not nearly as difficult as it may seem. Simple intuition may be the most compelling evidence.

The Gold Watch - _Creation Model_

Hans created timepieces. As a young man he made ordinary sundials. He later built hourglasses and water timers. And he fashioned all kinds of clocks... magnificent grandfather clocks, pretty little anniversary clocks... clocks of every shape and size. But his most prized creation was a watch.

Hans worked on details of his gold watch for many years. Day after day he labored over design - sizing every gear, calculating every small weight and detailing the exquisite artwork. Meticulous care went into the manufacture of each piece. Tiny gears were microscopically measured, formed and polished for precision. The balance wheel was carefully calibrated ensuring maximum accuracy. The spring, the casing, the face, the crystal... every detail was crafted to create the most "perfect" timepiece ever. Finally, when the last gear was delicately placed, the polished crystal gently set and the gold band lovingly attached... Hans marvelled at the beauty and precision of his masterpiece. He realized, however, that he was still holding just a beautiful ornament. Then Hans began to wind the watch. The sound began...
"Tick, Tick, Tick". The ornament had become a timepiece.

The Gold Watch - _Evolution Model_

Billions of years ago, the earth was far more favorable to "manufacturing" than today. Surrounding the earth was a sea of "ooze", richly laden with the precise elements to create timepieces. Bits of gold, bits of silica, even bits of paint.

Years and years went by. Then the inevitable happened. Bits of metal were joined together by volcanic heat. Amazingly, metal molecules bonded in the exact way needed to create intricate gears and balance wheels. As the parts tumbled in the "ooze", delicate polishing occurred: Precision polishing in the exact way to produce a perfectly calibrated timepiece. Then, molecules of black paint formed together in exact patterns to create numbers. And they coincidentally landed on a surface randomly covered with pure white paint. As years continued to pass, eventually gears, wheels, a face, a crystal and a beautifully engraved band came together to form an exquisite gold watch... a product of the right mix of materials and billions of years. It was beautiful. It was complete and meticulously formed. It was perfect in every way. Almost... It still needed someone to wind it.

An absurd example? The Gold Watch we laughingly and quickly recognize as a creation, is _far more primitive_ than the simplest life-form. Living cells are much smaller, and perform much more complex functions much faster, including:

- ❑ Self-diagnosis
- ❑ Growth
- ❑ Healing
- ❑ Reproduction

Why is it so difficult to accept that <u>life is created</u>?

Observation..

The public seems to think *fossil evidence* supports evolution. It doesn't. Over 100 years ago, Darwin hoped fossils would someday provide transitional evidence. Now, millions of fossils later, the evidence actually suggests creation, not evolution.

> ### Fossil Evidence [4, 17, 21, 22-24, 27]

Nobody denies existence of fossils. Although some reject fossil dating. (Carbon dating and other methods have important limitations and may be prone to error.) However, accuracy of dating is *not* the major issue in analyzing fossil evidence.

Millions upon millions of fossils have been recovered since Darwin. Moreover many hundreds of thousands of fossil species have been identified. Yet with all that evidence, *not one* single "missing link" clearly demonstrates the transition from one reproductive species to another. Why? It seems obvious that none ever existed.

Researchers have to "stretch" evidence to attempt to build a case for evolution. Such evidence includes hoaxes and mistakes (see insert), and creating arguments regarding "Common Design" and "Body Part Remnants" (p. 7). One "Common Design" fossil example used in a misleading way, is the "Archaeopteryx", a flying bird that has teeth and tiny claws on its wings. This extinct bird has nothing really unusual. Several birds and reptiles have teeth. Some birds even have claws on wings serving various functions (ostriches, the touraco and the hoatzin). Horses are another common evolutionary example with speculation that the size of horses "evolved" and early toes "evolved" to hoofs. This faulty thinking has been proliferated in many textbooks. However, analysis of selective breeding indicates considerable size variation exists within the original DNA code for horses. Likewise, fossils of multi-toed "horses" are actually a species form of the coney. The coney is not a horse at all.

What DO fossils tell us? They actually provide very strong support for creation. Fossil experts have found that new species appeared suddenly and abruptly... as if they were created "from nothing" (just as the *Bible* claims). Not one fossil has been found suggesting the lengthy process of evolution.

In summary, the fossil "evidence" hoped for by Darwin was never discovered. Fossils instead indicate creation of many distinctly different species.

Neanderthal... a Man? [22]

It was once thought that the Neanderthal was a man. But recent genetic DNA research indicates the chromosomes DO NOT match those of humans. They DO match those of bi-pedal primates (apes).

Tools? The use of crude tools by Neanderthal does not mean they were human. Many animals including birds, fish and mammals use "tools".

Shelter? If Neanderthal created shelters, likewise, it does not imply they were human. Many animals (beavers, birds, bees) also construct shelters.

Religion? There is NO evidence that Neanderthal practiced any form of worship or religion. Interestingly, that is the primary way the *Bible* separates Man from animals.

upports Creation

Observation of *mutations* (required for evolution) and *experimentation*... also refute evolution and support creation.

Mutations [17, 20, 27]

For evolution to "work" a mechanism had to be found that could create change. Fish scales don't "just turn into feathers". Evolutionists developed the theory that favorable mutations created change (perhaps due to radiation, which scientists know can cause mutation). However mutations are almost always *destructive*. In thousands of observed cases, only a few viral/bacterial mutations have contributed favorably to its species.

A second problem is the passing of mutations to successive generations. Mutations are not inherited by offspring (except in a few bacteria) making it an unacceptable mechanism.

Finally, a large number of favorable mutations would usually be necessary to have any value. Feathers, for example, would be useless unless wings were covered AND other coincidental changes occurred (e.g. wing formation, lightweight bone structure and a brain that "knew" how to fly).

Hoaxes and Mistakes [17, 27]

The intensive search for "missing links" has resulted in a number of mistakes and even fraud. Unfortunately, some still are in publication today.

Piltdown Man - A deliberate hoax. An ape jaw attached to a human skull was stained to look old.

Java Man - The discoverer later rejected it stating that a human and ape were just found in proximity.

Peking Man - Tools and human bones were found near the apes whose brains they were eating (monkey brains are still eaten in China).

Nebraska Man - An entire person (and family) was envisioned from a single tooth... a tooth that later proved to have come from a pig.

Lucy - Reclassified as an extinct ape.

Ramapithecus - A jaw and teeth were eventually dismissed as early human in origin (an Orangutan).

Experimentation [2, 17, 27]

The famous Stanley Miller experiment, that supposedly created building blocks of life, is still contained in many textbooks. In reality, this (and other experiments) do more to show the impossibility of random life formation, than to support evolution. Despite a carefully contrived environment (which did NOT correctly simulate early earth) only 2 of the (approximately) 50 "building blocks" were produced. And despite years of attempts to perfect the experiment, the quantities produced were always insignificant, the destructive by-product (tar) was always far too high and new problems showing life could NOT have evolved were exposed (pp. 16 - 17). A boast that Miller's experiment "proves" evolution, would be like someone randomly producing a "period" of black ink, then claiming it to be proof that the *Encyclopedia Britannica* randomly evolved. Hence, the greatest, most contrived efforts of man have not come remotely close to producing even the simplest of life components randomly. Now, biochemistry breakthroughs can "prove" why (see pp. 16, 20-21).

EVOLUTION

☐ 1 ☐ 2 ☐ 3 ☐ 4 ☐ 5 Virtually　　Equally　　Virtually Impossible　Probable　Certain	Anything not having a "natural" explanation is impossible. Creation is excluded "by definition".
☐ 1 ☐ 2 ☐ 3 ☐ 4 ☐ 5 Virtually　　Equally　　Virtually Impossible　Probable　Certain	Fossils show evolution. Formed billions of years ago, they reveal a long evolutionary period. Similar body parts of creatures show ancestry.
☐ 1 ☐ 2 ☐ 3 ☐ 4 ☐ 5 Virtually　　Equally　　Virtually Impossible　Probable　Certain	Radiation produced billions of favorable mutations... enabling creatures to better survive. Mutations were passed on to offspring.
☐ 1 ☐ 2 ☐ 3 ☐ 4 ☐ 5 Virtually　　Equally　　Virtually Impossible　Probable　Certain	The Stanley Miller experiment "proved" the building blocks of life could have been duplicated in conditions somewhat similar to the early earth's conditions.
☐ 1 ☐ 2 ☐ 3 ☐ 4 ☐ 5 Virtually　　Equally　　Virtually Impossible　Probable　Certain	Evolutionists hope an infinite time frame could allow the "impossible" to happen.
☐ 1 ☐ 2 ☐ 3 ☐ 4 ☐ 5 Virtually　　Equally　　Virtually Impossible　Probable　Certain	Evolutionists are "forced" to reject the evidence of "proof" of General Relativity.
☐ 1 ☐ 2 ☐ 3 ☐ 4 ☐ 5 Virtually　　Equally　　Virtually Impossible　Probable　Certain	Evolutionists are "forced" to reject the evidence of "proof" of General Relativity and hope an infinite time frame could allow the "impossible" to happen.
☐ 1 ☐ 2 ☐ 3 ☐ 4 ☐ 5 Virtually　　Equally　　Virtually Impossible　Probable　Certain	The "Big Bang" reveals how God was inconsequential in the creation process and indicates billions of years since earth began.
☐ 1 ☐ 2 ☐ 3 ☐ 4 ☐ 5 Virtually　　Equally　　Virtually Impossible　Probable　Certain	Evolutionists reject anything supernatural (e.g. outside time and space dimensions).

TOTAL RATING

CREATION

Creation is obvious from observing the vast complexity of life compared to any machine. A God in "extra dimensions" can work miracles.	☐1 ☐2 ☐3 ☐4 ☐5 Virtually Equally Virtually Impossible Probable Certain
Fossils support creation and deny evolution. *Abupt appearances* of distinct species occurred. NO missing links. Inadequate time for evolution.	☐1 ☐2 ☐3 ☐4 ☐5 Virtually Equally Virtually Impossible Probable Certain
Never have favorable mutations been produced in an "evolutionary" sense nor have they been passed on to offspring. Creation is consistent with observations	☐1 ☐2 ☐3 ☐4 ☐5 Virtually Equally Virtually Impossible Probable Certain
Experimentation supports creation. Even contrived environments produced far more killers of life building blocks. Almost none were created.	☐1 ☐2 ☐3 ☐4 ☐5 Virtually Equally Virtually Impossible Probable Certain
Evolution becomes "scientifically impossible" when the precision structure of cells of life are considered. Knowledgeable biochemists reject evolution. Creation is consistent with facts.	☐1 ☐2 ☐3 ☐4 ☐5 Virtually Equally Virtually Impossible Probable Certain
Evolution becomes "scientifically impossible" when laws of physics are considered. Knowledgeable physicists reject evolution. Creation is consistent with facts.	☐1 ☐2 ☐3 ☐4 ☐5 Virtually Equally Virtually Impossible Probable Certain
Evolution becomes "scientifically impossible" when laws of probability are considered. Few knowledgeable applied mathematicians or experts in probability accept evolution.	☐1 ☐2 ☐3 ☐4 ☐5 Virtually Equally Virtually Impossible Probable Certain
Breakthroughs, including the "Big Bang" literally "prove" creation. With limitations of time, matter and space, evolution is absolutely absurd. God was a necessity.	☐1 ☐2 ☐3 ☐4 ☐5 Virtually Equally Virtually Impossible Probable Certain
The supernatural evidence in the *Bible* makes it a reliable source of information including creation... which agrees with the scientific record.	☐1 ☐2 ☐3 ☐4 ☐5 Virtually Equally Virtually Impossible Probable Certain

TOTAL RATING

Microbiology..

The more we learn about the precision of living cells, the more obvious it is that life was created. Decades ago, little was known about complexity and structure of cells. David Hume and contemporaries of Darwin thought cells were just 'blobs' of protoplasm. Today we know better. Advances in microbiology, biochemistry, cybernetics and computer technology have forever changed our understanding.

Complexity of Living Cells [1, 2, 20]

Consider the vast system of just a single living cell. It's like an entire modern factory squeezed into a space one thousandth the size of the period at the end of this sentence. Then consider billions of factories (cells) all coordinated together. The functions of the human body are *far* beyond the most complex city.

So vast is the information routinely managed by the human body, it is beyond comprehension: Vision, blood clotting, digestion... or imagination, creativity, reproduction. If the information in a single human body were written in books, it would fill the Grand Canyon. Not once - but *fifty* times over.[2]

Biochemistry Rejects Evolution [1, 2, 17]

Biochemistry - the molecular level of microbiology - demonstrates that evolution could not possibly happen. Darwin and others did not have today's breakthrough knowledge: That intricate molecular biochemical "machines" perform complex functions such as vision, blood clotting and digestion. These machines are not simple "evolutionary steps" in plasma, but huge leaps in molecular design. Leaps that are impossible by random process. Evolutionists ignore this area. Even scientists wanting to reject creation see the impossibility of evolution (ref. 1).

Complexity of biochemical design is one area that now seems impossible for evolution to surmount. At the molecular level, random mutation would have had to have billions of favorable adaptations... all in a specific way... all at once.

Interdependence is another insurmountable barrier for biochemical evolution. For example, an eye requires many precise interdependent chemical systems to work. It's inconceivable that millions of changes randomly occurred instantaneously.

Life Molecule Development Steps [17, 20]

Development of protein chains (part of DNA, RNA) is NOT simple and NOT random.

1. Amino acids selected [Must have correct orientation - right/left handed].
2. LIFE SPECIFIC amino acids sorted, with incorrect ones rejected.
3. Correct amino acids bonded into short chains.
4. Hundreds of short chains bonded to specified length.
5. Chains with "sensible" order/instructions selected [e.g. no random "noise"].

Harold Morowitz[20] estimated the probability of all these steps randomly occurring for the *simplest living cell* to be: 1 in $10^{100,000,000,000}$... Like winning 1.4 million consecutive lotteries.

upports Creation

Microbiology now has defined many major barriers to evolution, not fully appreciated a few decades ago. The barriers involve the highly complex amino acid selection (prior page), the problem of a hostile environment - more likely to destroy than allow evolution, and the overall problem of programming information in the first place.

Amino Acid Selection - Chirality [2, 17, 20]

A number of very specific selection criteria have to be met to produce DNA. One of the most difficult to reconcile is chirality (right-left handedness). All amino acids are either right handed or left handed. To survive, a DNA chain must be made up of hundreds of *"pure" left handed amino acids* (capable of bonding to a different chain of *"pure" right handed nucleotides* - protein enzymes). *A single error* in either chain *makes it useless.* Yet attempts to produce amino acids always result in *equal* proportions of right/left kinds... so random selection of only the right-handed ones is virtually impossible. No method of correctly separating orientation has been found.

Environmental Barriers to Evolution [2]

Random development of a DNA molecule would be impossible even if conditions of early earth were perfect. But conditions were far from perfect. Problems include:

Oxygen - Oxygen destroys the chemical building blocks of life (either on land or under water). This led evolutionists to speculate that the early atmosphere was oxygen-free. However if so, then there would have been no protective ozone layer. Any DNA and RNA bonds would be destroyed by UV radiation. Either way, oxygen is a major problem. (Some evidence suggests early earth had much oxygen[2]).

Water - Everytime a nucleotide is added in the construction of a molecule of DNA, a molecule of water is released. The process is reversible. In chemistry, a reaction will *not naturally* proceed in a direction that produces a product already in abundance. Because water is produced, it would be impossible for DNA to form in water (as proposed by "ocean-vent" or primordial soup theories).

Toxic Waste - Tar is the major bi-product (by far) in all experiments producing simple amino acids. Tar would be deadly to proper functioning of DNA/RNA.

> ### Imagine...
>
> If a computer randomly typed letters and spaces on a page, how long would it take to produce ONE page accurately describing someone? All words must be spelled correctly. Sentences must be complete and grammar perfect. It would take a long time even at a rate of a page a second.
>
> Now imagine that any letter has a 50% chance of being upside down - one of which would destroy the page. At a page a second, it would take more than 10 billion years just to get a page of all upright letters (like flipping a coin - 5000 "heads").
>
> This example is analogous to the evolutionary model of random events creating the first DNA... except for one thing: Instead of *one page*, we would need to create *500,000 pages* to produce a single DNA molecule.

Physics..

Recent breakthroughs in physics offer serious-minded scientists virtually irrefutable evidence that there is a creator. Most of this new evidence appeared in the 1990's and is still unknown to much of the world. It has caused many of the world's leading scientists (including Stephen Hawking, Michael Turner and Carlos Frenk) to reconsider the existence of a God of the universe.

General Relativity [2, 20, 21, 25, 27]

Einstein's theory of General Relativity is the basis for some of the strongest evidence. General Relativity is a fundamental mathematical law that describes the space, matter, time and motions of the universe. In Einstein's time it was proven only to a "90% confidence level". That means using verification available at the time, there was a 90% chance that the equation was accurate. Now, due to many additional verification experiments, that confidence has risen to at least 99.99999999999999999999% (it is essentially fact). What does it mean? It means:

> ### General Relativity "Proves" that...
> ### Time, Matter and Space had a Beginning.

Understanding this is beyond most human beings. How can we conceive of No time? No matter? No space? It requires a perception of dimensions beyond time and space (p. 9). Convincing a non-physicist that this is true is often futile and depends on an individual's capacity to accept facts suggested by evidence of things beyond what we can perceive. Naturally, the world at large will be slow to understand this. But at this point in time, many of the most brilliant physicists, including many atheists, are trying to reconcile the implications...

> ### A Beginning Implies a Creator.

COBE Satellite - This space probe sent back our first "view" of the edges of the universe. Essentially, its data confirmed General Relativity and the existence of a Creator. News flashes around the world (in 1992) proclaimed the evidence: "The discovery of the century, if not of all time" (Stephen Hawking), and "Like looking at God" (George Smoot, Berkeley). Even prime time news carried the story (ABC's Ted Koppel). Unfortunately, the public generally did not recognize the significance of the scientific discovery and essentially ignored it.

Hubble Telescope - This space telescope provided unprecedented views of the heavens (it was the first telescope outside of earth's distorting atmosphere). Like the COBE Satellite, in the early 1990's it added vast support for General Relativity and to our understanding of the cosmos. [Note: see references]

Analysis of General Relativity

Discoveries in the 1990's finally provides adequate, solid evidence to calculate the actual mathematical probability of evolution. Not surprisingly, the probability of evolution is absurd from a strictly scientific and statistical viewpoint (p. 20).

upports Creation

Entropy - 2nd Law Thermo.[2, 17, 20, 21, 27]

Entropy states that the Universe tends to move from a state of order to disorder. Springs unwind, gases disperse, your desk becomes disorganized. Input of energy is required to return to a state of organization (e.g. winding of a spring, purposely collecting a gas or reorganizing your desk). There is NO mechanism of physics that would *organize initial life cells* - entropy implies the opposite.

Evolution requires inconceivable random development of order from chaos. It implies that the most complex machine we have ever observed (the human body) is a product of *billions of aberrations* of an entropy law that is accepted as fact. *That is a stretch of faith*. Purposeful creation fits the entropy law (p. 11).

Ironically, a "more scientific" viewpoint would be to consider the evidence within the laws of physics... to recognize that a creator purposefully input energy (and design) to develop the most incredibly complex order imaginable - life.

1st Law of Thermodynamics [2]

The first law of thermodynamics states that energy and matter can not be created or destroyed (it can just be converted from one to the other). Now, neither evolution nor creation seem to violate this law. However there is the nagging problem of the *original* universe. How did the sum total of matter and energy come to be in the first place? Evolution provides no answer (it just "was..."). Creation, specifically the *Bible*, clearly tells how a supernatural God (outside time and space) created the universe, life and then "rested". Nothing new was created.

Infinite Time - Evolutionist Hope

The only remaining hope for evolution is infinite time. Presumably infinite time and an infinite "number of events" could make anything conceivable. Now however, this last hope of evolution has been proven false by many of the same people hoping evolution is true. A few scientists are scrambling to propose other theories or to discredit Einstein. *Rejection of God has become very "unscientific".*

Is Light Slowing Down?

If the earth is only about 10,000 years old (Young Earth view) then how is it we see stars 5 billion light years away? It would imply at least a 5 billion year old universe. Some have proposed that speed of light has been slowing down.

Most physicists would scoff at the idea that light is slowing down. Many vital relationships depend on a constant speed of light. The most familiar is $E=mc^2$. If light were twice as fast in the time of Abraham, the sun would incinerate life.

A God that could create the universe, could alter physics, or provide protection. It's a decision of faith. Did God work *within* the laws of physics (Old Earth)? Or did he work *outside* them (Young Earth)? (p 8).

Probability..

General Relativity combined with several recent discoveries by the COBE satellite and *Hubble* telescope now allow scientists to accurately measure and calculate:

1. The <u>size</u> of the universe,

2. The <u>amount of matter</u> contained in it, and

3. The <u>amount of time</u> since the (apparent) beginning of the universe.

Combining these measurements with our knowledge of microbiology (biochemistry) and the components necessary to create a living cell, we can calculate the likelihood of random development of a cell as claimed by evolution. As a result, most microbiologists, physicists and experts in applied mathematics and statistics (that know about the findings) now reject evolution.

The Age & Size of the Universe [2, 20, 21]

The actual "edges of the universe" were defined and "announced" in 1992 by a team of scientists led by astronomer George Smoot from the University of California, Berkeley. Smoot's COBE satellite project had provided many discoveries about the nature of the universe and formation of galaxies (what the space probe was designed to do). Now that we are accurately mapping the edges (with millions of data points added every year since) we have more assurance of the actual size and age than ever before.

The latest findings have provided the following calculations of age and size:

How Much Proof... is Really PROOF?

If someone *told you he could* pick the winning lottery number, *then did*... you might be impressed. Odds are, maybe, one in ten million (or 1 in 10^7). Does that "prove" the person has Divine knowledge? Maybe or maybe not... though it is VERY VERY impressive. Now suppose he did it twice in a row? (One chance in a hundred thousand billion... 10^{14}) It suddenly seems obvious he had "special" information.

From a practical standpoint, scientists have determined that anything beyond one chance in 10^{50} is beyond reason... essentially impossible or absurd (Like someone correctly picking the lottery 7 times in a row)... Odds of evolution are *FAR LESS LIKELY* than winning <u>thousands</u> of lotteries. Statistically, evolution is "impossible".

Age
of Universe

10^{17} seconds

Size
of Universe

5×10^9 light year radius

upports Creation

A combination of findings including those from the COBE program and the *Hubble Space Telescope*, also allow us to calculate, with reasonable accuracy, the amount of matter in the universe. Such calculations indicate:

Matter
in the Universe

10^{84} baryons*

* A baryon is a common example of sub-atomic particles (e.g. proton).

Probability of Evolution Start

The probability of randomly producing a single living cell can now be calculated. The maximum number of conceivable interactions between sub-atomic particles is 10^{20} events per second. Combining maximum time, maximum matter and maximum number of interactions we can calculate the total number of events possible since the beginning of time:

$$10^{17} \quad X \quad 10^{84} \quad X \quad 10^{20} \quad = \quad 10^{121}$$

| Time | Particles | Events/second | Total Events |

The total number of "events" required to produce a single living (reproductive) cell can be determined based on the necessary DNA building blocks (p. 16 - 17).

Events necessary to produce a single living cell** $= 10^{100,000,000,000}$

$$\text{Probability of Evolutionary Start} = \frac{10^{121}}{10^{100,000,000,000}} = \frac{1}{10^{99,999,999,879}} = 0$$

Do New Findings Mean "Young Earth" is Wrong?

Not necessarily. Although most scientists will likely feel the Old Earth Biblical view has more substantial evidence than the Young Earth view (p. 8). Yet, as indicated before, a Creator of the universe could certainly work outside the laws of physics (which he created) or create things in an existent state of age.

The important issue is NOT whether "Young Earth" or "Old Earth" is correct... but that *evolution could not possibly have happened at all.* To a scientist or statistician, it makes virtually NO difference whether the earth is ten thousand years old or ten billion. Ten billion years is still FAR TOO SHORT for a single living cell to develop... let alone the complex parade of changes that evolution requires. *ALL new discoveries* ... including "Big Bang" evidence... *support creation and disprove evolution.*

** Harold Morowitz, molecular biologist.

Cosmology..

Uninformed popular opinion presumes the more we discover about the heavens, more evidence there is contradicting the *Bible*, God and the creation account. Nothing could be further from the truth. Millions of pieces of data supporting the *Bible* are added daily. This includes more mapping of the universe, further proving General Relativity (along with it's "proof" of creation - pp. 18 - 21). Growing evidence also further reveals a remarkably fine-tuned universe clearly pointing to a unique planet earth.

> **Evidence: Large and Small**
>
> Breakthrough developing rapidly in the BOTH the largest space... the heavens (cosmology), and the smallest space... atoms (biochemistry) are confirming the God of the *Bible* more than ever before.

Claims that suggest a "likelihood" of another planet "earth" are not based on consideration of the parameters (and probabilities) necessary for a life-support planet. Unfortunately, large numbers can be misleading... "billions of stars" or "billions of planets". They seem to favor another "earth". *But odds of meeting all criteria necessary to support earth's life-forms are even much more remote.*

The Uniqueness of Planet Earth [20]

Every year astrophysicists are discovering additional specific and delicate criteria necessary for the life forms found on earth. Consider just the events of the first "two days" of the *Genesis* creation event alone (creation of the proper atmosphere, and the establishment of the hydrological cycle). Factors necessary to achieve *just the two criteria* are estimated to be one in a hundred trillion trillion (one in 10^{26}). Assuming the number of planets anticipated in the Universe, 10^{22} (considered "generous"), the chance of another life support planet is remote. By adding the other factors needed for life... it becomes absurd. The following lists only a few examples in a list of over sixty criteria determined to be *critical* for life on earth:

Life could NOT exist if <u>any one</u> of the following were true:

❑ Slower Rotation of earth ❑ Smaller earth ❑ Earth's crust thinner
❑ Faster Rotation of earth ❑ Larger earth ❑ Earth's crust thicker
❑ 2-5% Further from sun ❑ Smaller moon ❑ Oxygen/Nitrogen ratio great
❑ 2-5% Closer to sun ❑ Larger moon ❑ Oxygen/Nitrogen ratio less
❑ 1% Change - sun light ❑ More than one moon ❑ Greater or lesser ozone

The Amazing "Timed" Collision [22]

Many scientists feel "certain" that a heavenly body half the size of Mars collided with the earth at precisely the right time in the earth's development (supported by cosmology). The collision "knocked" much CO_2 out of it's atmosphere - averting a life-preventing "runaway greenhouse effect" and allowing the right atmospheric chemistry. It also increased the speed of rotation (important). The moon was formed from part of the colliding body, and became a vital element in stabilizing the earth's axis and rotation - creating the environment for life. *Odds of this event happening in such a precise way <u>without God</u>, are beyond reason.*

Supports Creation

Cosmology (and other fields of applied physics) provide considerable data to support General Relativity - and hence strengthen many claims that refute evolution. Likewise, research of the heavens defines the complex fine-tuning of the universe and shows evidence of Divine design (p. 22). However, public fascination with "extra-terrestrials" combined with speculation and misinformation fueled by the media, gives cosmology an additional role... that of providing wisdom to a world seemingly anxious to find advanced life elsewhere.

Life on Mars? Other Planets? [20, 24]

Will we ever find life from Mars? Probably yes. Other planets? Probably yes. But not the kind of life the world is looking for. Cosmologists have known for years that life escapes earth's environment and travels to other planets. Several varieties of tiny microbes have been found in the upper atmosphere (since 1960). Solar "wind" (photons from the sun) can launch such small life (.2 to 1.0 microns) into outer space. Several forms of microbe species can actually live in outer space for many years... long enough to reach Mars, and even beyond.

Furthermore, calculations indicate a meteor colliding with earth can launch boulders into outer space. (A meteor large enough to create a 60 mile creator is necessary, yet such meteors have collided with earth in the past.) Of rocks ejected, about 29% would strike Venus, 2% will hit Mercury, and less that 2% will hit Mars and Jupiter. One rock would even hit Saturn. So it's easy to understand why remnants of microscopic life will probably be found someday on other planets. But it will probably consist of only the smallest of life forms from earth.

The "Mars" Rock [24]

Does the famous "Mars Rock" of 1996 (ALLH84001) contain life? Probably not. Attention from the press and politicians seems to reflect more about public interest than good science. For starters, while visual photos seemed to resemble compounds created by organisms, the same material can also be produced without life... a more likely scenario given that the carbonates were (probably) formed above the upper temperature limit for biological carbonates.

The size of the find also appears too small (100 times smaller than the smallest fossils). It likely contains less than a hundred million atoms, which is too small to sustain life.

Aliens From Outer Space?

Some have suggested aliens from outer space created life. Evidence of aliens is highly speculative at best. Even if aliens do exist, who created them? A Creator outside of time and space would still be necessary.

Why are some quick to accept such weak evidence when abundant evidence of the God of the *Bible* exists? Evidence based on historical facts. Evidence based on the verifiable supernatural communication within the *Bible* [see ref. p. 28]. Evidence based on millions of testimonies. Is something else drawing rational minds and hearts away from the obvious?

Biblical Accuracy.

Suppose you had a very wise mentor. He provided you information of many things with incredibly perfect accuracy. Not only was his knowledge of history amazing, but he knew facts no one else knew and predicted the future without error. He precisely predicted such milestones as the development of the computer and the fall of Communism. He told you the exact day Nixon would resign... years before Nixon was born. And he gave you winning lottery numbers dozens of times (making you very grateful and wealthy). Your wise mentor was never, <u>NEVER</u> wrong. How would you respond if he told you how the earth began?

The *Bible* is such a "mentor". Incredible as it is, the *Bible* has been perfectly accurate and predicted events much more spectacular without ever being wrong. Uninformed scholars debate this without knowledge of the real evidence. For example, such publications as *Time Magazine* (Oct. 28, 1996, p. 76) stated that: "...*Genesis* long, long ago crumbled under the weight of science, notably Darwin's theory of natural selection". *How can such a prominent magazine use information so out-of-date?* The informed scientific community (although often rejecting God) now recognizes breakthrough evidence in physics, astronomy and biochemistry - and begrudgingly, discusses God. This evidence takes years to filter down to the academic level because of roadblocks of "religious implications". Unfortunately, until others are "taught", faulty information is perpetuated in the general media.

The facts are: The *Bible* has "More sure marks of authenticity than any (secular writing) ever..." (Sir Isaac Newton - see p.1). The *Bible* "proves" its authorship by God with evidence far beyond human perception including:

❑ **Scientific Insights** - Information about science and the world - written centuries before man discovered them. Dozens of amazing scientific insights are contained in the *Bible* (ref: p. 28).

❑ **Prophecy Miracles** - The future foretold, in some cases many centuries before events. Every Biblical prophecy that could be verified - hundreds of them - has been verified as accurate. (ref: p. 28).

❑ **Concealed Evidence** - Evidence of Divine Design that shows patterns of words, models and other information that would be impossible to humanly create. (ref: p. 28).

Moses... God-Inspired? Or... Lottery Winner?

The account of creation written by Moses over 3,000 years ago is 100% accurate in the order of events (p. 25). If we break the account into 10 simple events, the odds of Moses correctly guessing ONLY THE CORRECT ORDER OF EVENTS is about one chance in 4 million... A little better than the odds of winning a state lottery.

Moses had no "science" to guide him. Creation accounts in holy books of other religions attest to vast misconceptions of creation at the time. Moreover, how did Moses know what events to "pick" in the first place?

Was Moses directed by God? Or was he essentially a "lottery winner"?

upports Creation

Thorough understanding of *Genesis* 1 requires considering the original Hebrew text. English translations can be misleading. For example: on day 4, verse 16 might imply that the sun and moon were created after the formation of plants... a problem for scientists. The actual Hebrew verb and tense used in conjunction with the words in Gen 1:1, correctly indicate the sun and moon "*became visible*" at the surface of the earth on day 4 (but were *previously created*).

Reviewing the *order of events* of creation shows the *Bible* is accurate as far as science can verify. It's important to notice the *vantage point* (frame of reference) of "God's spirit"... hovering over the waters [Gen 1:2].

> ## *Events of Creation (confirmed by science)*[19, 24]

1. ***Heavenly bodies created*** [Gen 1:1] - The earth was initially covered with a thick layer of gas and dust *not allowing light to penetrate*. This is probably a standard condition of planets of the earth's mass and temperature. The initial conditions described in the *Bible* are accepted by science: Dark, formless and void.

2. ***"Let there be light"*** [Gen 1:3] - The atmosphere became translucent to allow *some* light to reach the surface of the water, a critical prerequisite for the introduction of life (and the process of photosynthesis).

3. ***Development of Hydrologic cycle***. [Gen 1:6] - The "perfect" conditions of temperature, pressure and distance from the sun would allow all forms of H_2O (ice, liquid and vapor) - all necessary for life.

4. ***Formation of land and sea*** [Gen 1:9-10] - Seismic and volcanic activity occur in the precise proportion to allow 30 percent of the surface to become and remain land. Scientists have determined this is the ideal ratio to promote the greatest complexity of life forms.

5. ***Creation of vegetation***. [Gen 1:11] - Light, water and large amounts of CO_2 set the stage for vegetation. This was the first life form.

6. ***Atmosphere transparency***. [Gen 1:14] - Plants gradually produced oxygen to a level of 21%. This (and other factors) caused a transparent atmosphere to form and permitted "Lights in the heavens" to become visible at the surface of the earth... marking day and night and seasons.

7. ***Creation of small sea animals and birds***. [Gen 1:20] - Scientists agree these were the first animal life forms of all classes discussed in the *Bible*.

8. ***Creation of land animals***. [Gen 1:24] - The final life-forms prior to Man were created: Quadrupeds and rodents.

9. ***Creation of Man***. [Gen 1:26] - Final life creation appearing on earth.

10. ***No additional Creation***. [Gen 2:2] - No unique creation has occurred since.

Common Questions

If Mankind is Created... What's Our Purpose?

The Creation miracle was accurately recorded thousands of years ago in the *Bible* - which contains other evidence of miraculous communication from God (see other references listed on p. 28). It also outlines Man's historical interaction with God, and Man's purpose: An eternal relationship with God, the Creator. A relationship with God does not depend on believing the entire *Bible* (although thorough investigation will reveal it's 100% accuracy). It *does depend* on knowing the **right God**, and having the **right relationship** with him. God came to earth in the human form of Jesus Christ, to communicate to humans and redeem them. Believing in Jesus and accepting him to be director of your life is all that is required.

How Can We Ensure the Right Relationship to Go to Heaven?

When Jesus said not all who use his name will enter heaven [Mt 7:21-23] he was referring to people who think using Christ's name along with rules and rituals is the key to heaven. A *relationship* with God is <u>NOT</u> based on rituals or rules. It's based on grace, forgiveness and the right relationship.

How to Have a Personal Relationship with God

1. **B**elieve that God exists and that he came to earth in the human form of Jesus Christ. [John 3:16; Rom 10:9]

2. **A**ccept God's free forgiveness of sins through the death and resurrection of Jesus Christ. [Eph 2:8-10; Eph 1:7-8]

3. **S**witch to God's plan for your life. [1 Pet 1:21-23; Eph 2:1-5]

4. **E**xpress desire for Christ to be director of your life. [Mt 7:21-27; 1 John 4:15]

Prayer for Eternal Life with God

"Dear God, I believe you sent your son, Jesus, to die for my sins so I can be forgiven. I'm sorry for my sins and I want to live the rest of my life the way you want me to. Please put your Spirit in my life to direct me. Amen."

Then What?

People who sincerely take the above steps become members of God's family of Believers. New freedom and strength is available through prayer and obedience to God's will. The new relationship can be strengthened by:

- ❑ Finding a *Bible*-based church that you like, and attend regularly.
- ❑ Setting aside some time each day to pray and read the *Bible*.
- ❑ Locating other Christians to spend time with on a regular basis.

God's Promises to Believers

<u>For Today</u>

But seek first his kingdom and his righteousness, and all these things *[e.g. things to satisfy all your needs]* will be given to you as well. Mt 6:33

<u>For Eternity</u>

Whoever believes in the Son has eternal life,
but whoever rejects the Son will not see life,
for God's wrath remains on him. John 3:36

Once we develop an eternal perspective, even the greatest problems on earth fade in significance.

References

Note: The author does not agree with *all* authors below on *all* viewpoints - some of which differ with each other. Each reference has some findings worthy of consideration. *("Test everything" - 1 Thes 5:21)*
"Primary Viewpoint" Codes: Y = Young Earth, O = Old Earth, A = Atheistic, Agnostic or Secular view

1   Behe, Michael, *Darwin's Black Box*, New York, NY: Simon & Scheuster, 1996. - A
2   Eastman, MD, Mark and Missler, Chuck, *The Creator Beyond Time and Space*, Costa Mesa, CA: The Word for Today, 1996.
3   *Encyclopedia Britannica*, Chicago, IL: 1993. - A
4   Gange, Dr. Robert, *A Scientist Looks at Creation*, Videotape, Cleveland, OH: Reel to Real & American Portrait Film, 1992. - O
5   Gish, Duane T., Ph.D., *Evolution: The Challenge of the Fossil Record*, El Cajon, CA: Creation-Life Publishers, 1986. - Y
6   Ham, Ken, The Lie - Evolution, El Cajon, CA: Creation-Life Publishers, 1987. - Y
7   Herbert, David, Charles Darwin's Religious Views, London, Onterio: Hersil Publishing, 1990.
8   Mc Dowell, Josh and Stewart, Don, *Answers to Tough Questions*, Wheaton, IL: Living Books, 1980.
10 Mc Dowell, Josh and Stewart, Don, *Reasons Skeptics should consider Christianity*, Wheaton, IL : Living Books, 1981.
11 Mc Dowell, Josh and Wilson, Bill, *A Ready Defense*, San Bernadino, CA: Here's Life Publishers, Inc., 1990.
12 Missler, Chuck, *Beyond Coincidence* Audio Tape, Coeur d'Alene, ID: Koinonia House Inc., 1994.
13 Missler, Chuck, *Beyond Perception*, Audio Tape, Coeur d'Alene, ID: Koinonia House Inc., 1994.
14 Missler, Chuck, *Beyond Time & Space*, Audio Tape, Coeur d'Alene, ID: Koinonia House Inc., 1994.
15 Missler, Chuck, *Genesis and the Big Bang*, Audio Tape, Coeur d'Alene, ID: Koinonia House Inc., 1994.
16 Morris, Henry M., *Men of Science- Men of God*, El Cajon, CA: Master Books, 1992. - Y
17 Morris, Henry M., Parker, Gary E., *What is Creation Science?*, El Cajon, CA: Master Books, 1987. - Y
18 Muncaster, Ralph O., *The Bible - Scientific Insights - Investigation of the Evidence*, Newport Beach, CA: Strong Basis to Believe, 1996.
19 Ross, Hugh, Ph.D., *Beyond the Cosmos*, Colorado Springs, CO: NAVPRESS, 1996. - O
20 Ross, Hugh, Ph.D., *The Creator and the Cosmos*, Colorado Springs, CO: NAVPRESS, 1993. - O
21 Ross, Hugh, Ph.D., *Creation and Time*, Colorado Springs, CO: NAVPRESS, 1994. - O
22 Ross, Hugh, Ph.D., *Facts & Faith*, Pasedena, CA: Reasons to Believe, Third Quarter, 1995. - O
23 Ross, Hugh, Ph.D., *Facts & Faith*, Pasedena, CA: Reasons to Believe, Second Quarter, 1996. - O
24 Ross, Hugh, Ph.D., *Facts & Faith*, Pasedena, CA: Reasons to Believe, Fourth Quarter, 1996. - O
25 Ross, Hugh, Ph.D., *The Fingerprint of God*, Orange, CA: Promise Publishing Co., 1989. - O
26 Stewart, Don, *The Bible and Science - Are They in Conflict?*, Spokane, WA: AusAmerica , 1993. - Y
27 Taylor, Paul S., *Origins Answer Book*, Mesa, AZ: Eden Communications, 1995 - Y

Investigation of the Evidence
by Ralph O. Muncaster

Jesus Christ Series

Jesus

> Evidence supporting the existence and role of Jesus Christ. History, archaeology and prophecy verifies reality of Jesus. Evidence supports Deity of Jesus and reviews his purpose.

First Easter

> Information about Jesus specific to the Resurrection, including analysis historical dating and events.

First Christmas

> Information about Jesus specific to the First Christmas. Popular misconceptions of the Magi, angels, the star, the date of Jesus' birth and other items are clarified with the actual facts.

The Bible Series

Bible - General Analysis

> Facts regarding the development of the *Bible*. Analyzes manuscript evidence, archaeological support, prophecies, scientific accuracy and "hidden evidence". Confirms the reliability of the *Bible*.

Bible - Prophecy Miracles

> Summarizes many of the 100% accurate, precision prophecies written in the *Bible*... centuries in advance.

Bible - Hidden Evidence

> Incredible hidden evidence that statistically "proves" Divine planning.

Bible - Scientific Insights

> Biblical scientific insights that were correct long before science was.

Bible - Archaeological Facts

> Discoveries that demonstrate Biblical accuracy... even when scholars were wrong.

Bible - Manuscript Reliability

> The amazing manuscript evidence: development, survival and history.

Other

Creation versus Evolution

> Analyzes the *Biblical* account of Creation relative to modern science, molecular biology and statistical analysis. Compares likelihood of Creation to probability of Evolution. Reviews the fossil record and describes proven hoaxes of anthropology... sometimes left uncorrected in books and articles, even today.